NEXT STOP
NEPTUNE

EXPERIENCING THE SOLAR SYSTEM

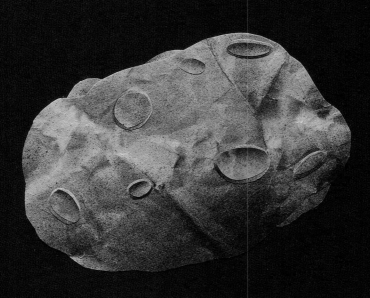

BY
ALVIN JENKINS
ILLUSTRATED BY
STEVE JENKINS

HOUGHTON MIFFLIN COMPANY   BOSTON 2004

It is very cold. The sun is just a bright star among thousands of others in a black sky. You take a step and soar 50 feet above the ground, which is covered with fine gray dust. Everywhere you look, the surface is marked with craters. Slowly, you float back down. When you finally land, the cloud of dust you stir up moves like a splash of water in slow motion, rising and then slowly falling back to the surface. You are standing on an asteroid.

No one has actually visited an asteroid. So far, humans have traveled to only one other place in the solar system — the moon. However, we've learned a lot about our neighbors in space by sending out unmanned probes and using powerful telescopes. One day, perhaps in the not-too-distant future, people may walk on Mars, visit a satellite of Jupiter, or hover above a comet. Until then, we know enough to imagine what it would be like to be there.

The solar system includes the sun, Earth and eight other planets, more than a hundred moons, thousands of asteroids, and millions of comets. In this book you will visit many of these places.

Before you imagine what it's like on another world, let's see how the solar system began and how it looks today.

A Star Is Born

About five billion years ago a vast cloud of gas and dust drifted through space. Gradually, as the cloud began to collapse, it became denser and hotter. The inner part of the cloud became so hot that it started to glow. Finally it ignited, becoming a star — our sun. The swirling cloud of dust and gas around this star began to condense and form solid particles. These particles clumped together to form pebbles, then larger boulder-size pieces. These rocky pieces continued to gather together within the cloud and eventually formed the nine planets and many of their moons.

The four planets closest to the sun — Mercury, Venus, Earth, and Mars — are rocky, because the heat of the nearby sun drove away most of their lighter gases. Farther out, where it was cooler, most of the gas remained, and planets formed with enormous atmospheres. Jupiter, Saturn, Uranus, and Neptune are called gas giants. Finally, there is Pluto, a small, rocky planet that may have been captured by the sun's gravity and become part of the solar system after the other planets formed. Between Mars and Jupiter are thousands of rocky objects that did not become part of a planet. These are the asteroids. Much farther away from the sun, beyond the planet Neptune, are millions of balls of ice and dirt just a few miles across — the comets.

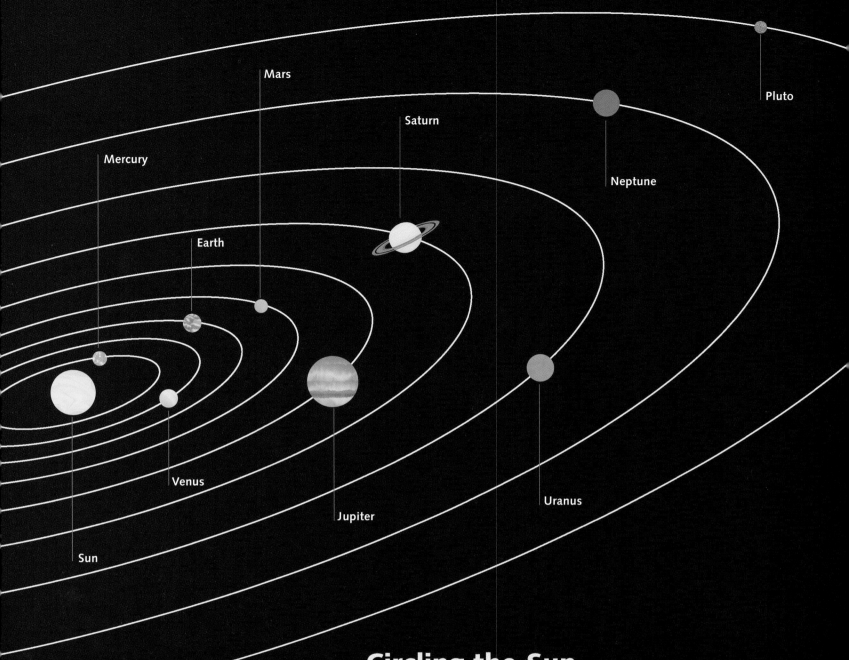

Pluto

Mars

Saturn

Neptune

Mercury

Earth

Venus

Uranus

Jupiter

Sun

Circling the Sun

The planets move in almost circular paths around the sun. This illustration shows their paths, or orbits, but not their actual spacing or size. Planets closer to the sun travel faster in their orbits, while those farther away travel more slowly. The outer planets also have much farther to go to circle the sun. The time it takes to make a full orbit, or complete trip around the sun, is called a year. A year on Mercury, the planet closest to the sun, lasts about three Earth months. Pluto, the most distant of the planets, takes 250 Earth years to complete one orbit. The planets also rotate, or spin, as they travel around the sun. A day on a planet is the length of time it takes the planet to rotate once.

Very Big, Very Empty

It's hard to realize how big the solar system really is. And because the planets are so small compared to the distances between them, it's hard to draw an accurate picture of the solar system. Imagine the sun shrunk to the size of a basketball. At this scale, the solar system is almost a mile and a half across, and all of its planets and moons together could be held in the palm of your hand. The solar system is mostly empty space.

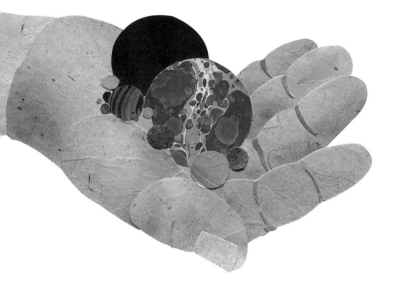

The Sun (a basketball)

Mercury (a peppercorn)
32 feet from the Sun

Venus (a pea)
60 feet from the Sun

Earth (a pea)
85 feet from the Sun

Mars (a kernel of corn)
130 feet from the Sun

The illustration across the bottom of the next four pages shows the scale of the solar system when the sun is the size of a basketball (at the lower left). Earth then becomes a pea about 85 feet away. Jupiter is a marble 450 feet away, and Pluto is the head of a pin 3,300 feet from the basketball-size sun.

Jupiter (a large marble)
450 feet from the Sun

Saturn (a large marble)
800 feet from the Sun

Uranus (a small marble)
1,600 feet from the Sun

Mercury

Venus

Earth and
Moon

Mars

Sun

Jupiter

Neptune (a small marble)
2,500 feet from the Sun

How Big?

The sun and planets are shown here at the same scale. In this picture, the sun is about five feet across.

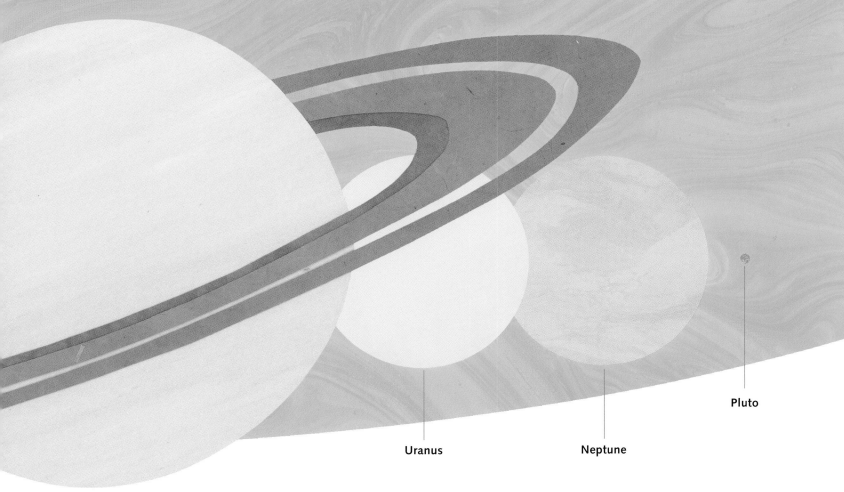

Saturn

Uranus

Neptune

Pluto

Pluto (the head of a pin)
3,300 feet from the sun

The sun is very bright and very, very hot. It is so hot that every material we know of would become vapor — turn to gas — before it could reach the sun's surface. From a few million miles away, you can see the sun rotate slowly. As you get closer, the surface churns and roils, like water boiling in a pan. Sunspots — large dark areas a few thousand miles across — move past below you.

A hundred thousand miles away, a spectacular column of brilliantly glowing gas shoots into space and falls back to the surface.

If you could dive into the sun, you'd find that there is nothing solid — it's made entirely of gas. Even so, the gas at the center of the sun is so dense that a drinking glass filled with it would weigh 75 pounds.

Sun

The sun is powered by nuclear reactions, the same as those that take place in a hydrogen bomb, but on a much larger scale. These reactions change hydrogen to helium and release great quantities of energy.

The temperature at the sun's surface is 10,000 degrees Fahrenheit. At the center of the sun, the temperature reaches 28 million degrees.

The sun is rotating, but it is turning faster at its equator than at its poles. This is possible because the sun isn't solid — it's made of gas. It takes 25 days for the sun to make one revolution at the equator, 34 days near the poles.

The sun is nearly a million miles in diameter. More than one million Earths could fit inside the sun. Here's what Earth and the sun look like at the same scale.

At the sun's surface, you would weigh about 27 times more than you do on Earth. What you feel as your weight is just the pull of gravity on your body, and the gravity of the sun is about 27 times greater than that of Earth. A person who weighs 90 pounds here would weigh almost 2,500 pounds on the sun.

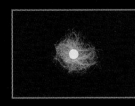

The sun is halfway through its life span as a regular star. In about four or five billion more years the sun will swell to an enormous size. The inner planets, including Earth, will be burned to a crisp. The sun will then blow off much of its atmosphere and collapse to form a small, hot star called a white dwarf.

Darker spots are often visible on the sun. These are "sunspots," regions slightly cooler than the rest of the surface. They last from several days to several weeks.

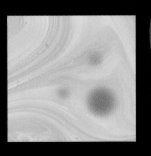

Occasionally the sun blasts tongues of hot gases high above the surface. These arches or columns can reach hundreds of thousands of miles into space. They are called prominences.

The sun is about 93 million miles from Earth. This distance is called an astronomical unit, or AU. If there were a road to the sun, it would take 177 years of nonstop driving at 60 miles per hour to get there.

You are standing on a bare, lifeless planet. The ground is hard and rocky and covered with gray dust. Everything is the same dull color. There are mountains in the distance and rugged terrain everywhere. There is no air, or atmosphere, on Mercury. On all sides are craters made by the impact of meteorites and asteroids. The sun, which has begun to set, looks much larger than it does on Earth. It is very hot. When the sun disappears from sight it will quickly become very dark and extremely cold — cold enough to freeze you almost instantly. But don't worry. It's only 88 days until sunrise!

Mercury

Of all the planets, only Pluto is smaller than Mercury. In fact, Mercury is not much larger than our moon.

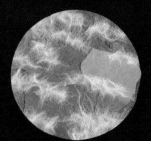 

Earth   Moon   Mercury

Mercury is the closest planet to the sun. When it is nearest to Earth during its orbit around the sun, it is still 60 million miles away from us.

You weigh much less on Mercury than on Earth. If you could jump three feet high on Earth, you'd be able to jump nine feet high on Mercury.

There is no atmosphere here. Without wind or water to erode the surface, Mercury hasn't changed much for millions of years.

Mercury has the widest temperature range of any planet. It reaches 800 degrees Fahrenheit (hot enough to melt lead) by noon, and falls as low as 280 degrees below zero just before dawn.

A day on Mercury lasts longer than a year. Because it rotates very slowly, sunrise to sunrise here is 176 Earth days, but a complete trip around the sun takes only 88 days.

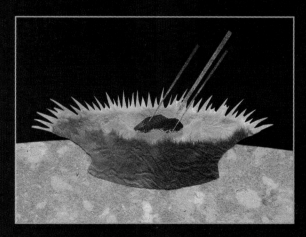

The surface of Mercury is covered with craters formed by the impact of comets and asteroids, mostly in the early years of the planet. An asteroid one mile in diameter, striking a rocky planet like Mercury with a typical speed of thirty miles per second (over 100,000 miles per hour), will blast a crater ten to fifteen miles in diameter.

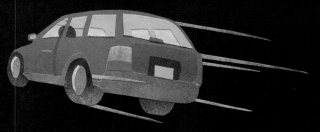

Driving at 60 miles per hour, it would take almost 110 years to reach Mercury.

As you approach Venus, you see a smooth, unbroken white cloud surface covering the entire planet. These clouds are several miles thick and are not made of water, like the clouds on Earth, but of tiny droplets of sulfuric acid. Below them there is a thick layer of haze. Going lower, you finally emerge from the haze into clear air about 20 miles above the surface of Venus. When you finally stand on solid ground, you find yourself in an extremely hot environment. It's hotter here than inside a fireplace with a roaring fire.

The ground is covered with slabs of rock, and barren mountains rise in the distance. Your vision seems blurred and warped by the thick atmosphere. It's very overcast during the day, and a soft yellowish light seems to come from everywhere. There are few shadows. Even at night the clouds glow with a dim light, and you can't see the sun or stars. If you lived on Venus, you might never know of Earth, or stars, or other planets, since they are always hidden by the clouds. The high temperatures and lack of water mean that no life, as we know it, can exist here.

Venus

Venus is closer to the sun than Earth, so it always appears near the sun in the sky and is visible only in the morning or evening. It is often called the Morning Star or the Evening Star, but the second planet from the sun is not a star, because it doesn't shine with its own light, but by reflected sunlight. At its brightest, Venus is brighter than all objects in the sky except the sun and the moon. Because of its beauty, this planet was named after the Greek goddess of love. In the past, many people believed that Venus might be covered with a giant ocean.

Venus is the only planet to rotate backward. On Venus the sun rises in the west and sets in the east.

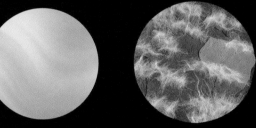

The Venusian atmosphere is very dense. The pressure here is 100 times that on the surface of Earth — the same pressure a submarine would experience at a depth of 3,000 feet in an ocean on Earth.

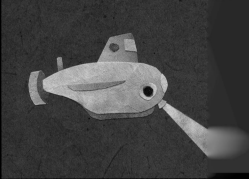

Venus is almost exactly the same size as Earth, and has about the same gravity. It is also nearby, in astronomical terms — as close as 25 million miles. Traveling at 60 miles per hour, it would take 50 years to travel this distance.

Many active volcanoes are found on Venus.

The high temperature on Venus is due to something called the greenhouse effect. The dense atmosphere allows the light from the sun to filter through the clouds and heat the surface. The energy radiated back from the surface, however, is almost completely blocked by the clouds, so the heat builds up. The same effect is present on Earth on a much smaller scale, but our atmosphere lets more heat escape.

Robot probes have landed on Venus's surface and sent back crude photographs. The probes worked for only about an hour until the high temperature destroyed them.

Approaching Earth from space, your first impression is of a beautiful blue ball hanging in a black sky. Getting closer, you see that the blue is mottled with white clouds and darker areas of land. Bright white regions of ice and snow can be seen at the top and bottom of Earth. Most of the planet is covered with water. The air is breathable, and in most places on the surface the temperature is comfortable — you are home. This is the only place in the solar system where you can survive without a sealed spacesuit. Anywhere else it is too hot or too cold, and either there is nothing to breathe or there's an atmosphere full of poisonous gases. Looking up from Earth on a dark, clear night you can see six other planets without a telescope: Mercury, Venus, Mars, Jupiter, Saturn, and Uranus.

Earth

Almost three quarters of Earth is covered with water, and the solid ground is always changing — continents move, mountains rise, and water, ice, and wind continually wear the surface down. As a result, Earth shows few of the scars of collisions that are seen on many other bodies in the solar system.

is not too hot or too cold — the average temperature is about 60 degrees — water can exist as a liquid here. This is important — as far as we know, life can exist only where there is liquid water.

Earth is constantly being bombarded by meteorites, which are bits of rock hurtling through space that collide with Earth. Many are only the size of a grain of sand. A few are much larger. If you've ever seen a shooting star, you were probably seeing a meteorite or a meteor, which is a meteorite that burns up before it reaches the surface. Occasionally Earth is struck by a comet or asteroid, an event that can affect everything living on the planet.

Earth spins on its axis and completes one revolution in twenty-four hours, or what we call one day. It makes a trip around the sun in just over 365 days, which we call a year. Every fourth year has an extra day added (a leap year, when February has 29 days) to make up for the extra time over 365 days.

Earth goes through natural cycles of warming and cooling. Right now, Earth is getting warmer, partly because the exhaust from cars and power plants, called greenhouse gases, trap the sun's heat in our atmosphere.

The seasons on Earth are caused by changes in the angle of the sunlight striking the surface. In the Southern Hemisphere the sun is directly overhead in the summer, strongly warming the surface. In the winter the sunlight falls at more of an angle, providing less warmth. The seasons are reversed in the Northern Hemisphere.

Driving at 60 miles per hour, day and night, it would take 17 days to travel the 25,000 miles around Earth at the equator.

You are standing in fine, soft, gray powder. The sun is very bright — an intense white disc. In the distance are mountains, craters, and a flat, smooth plain. Taking a step, you leave the ground and soar several feet before landing. There is no atmosphere. The most striking thing you see is the huge blue-green ball hovering in the black sky: Earth.

Moon

The moon looks mottled — patterned with light and dark areas — because of the many craters created by falling meteorites. The large smooth areas on the moon were created by gigantic lava flows that occurred billions of years ago.

A "day" on the moon has about 15 Earth days of sunlight followed by 15 days of night.

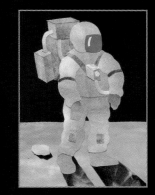

There were six landings on the moon by Apollo spacecraft, and twelve astronauts have explored the surface.

The moon and Earth at the same scale.

Seven of the nine planets have moons. Moons revolve around their planet, just as the planets revolve about the sun. Earth and Pluto each have only one moon. Venus and Mercury have none, and all the others have more than one. Moons are always smaller than their planets, but they vary greatly in size.

On the moon you weigh only about one sixth as much as on Earth, so if you can jump three feet on Earth, you'll be able to jump eighteen feet on the moon.

Astronomers believe that the moon was formed more than four billion years ago when a Mars-size body collided with Earth. A large amount of material from both Earth and the colliding body was blasted into orbit and came together to form the moon.

The moon is much closer to Earth than any other body in space, about 240,000 miles away. To drive to the moon at 60 miles per hour would take 167 days, or about five months. The Earth, the moon, and the distance between them are shown at accurate scale below.

Here you are in a sandy, rocky landscape that looks a lot like a desert on Earth. The air is thin and very cold. The wind whips the fine red soil into fast-moving dust clouds. In the distance a mountain rises above a steep cliff. The land nearby is gently rolling, and has an orange color. The sky is yellowish because of the dust in the air. Here and there are craters of various sizes, and you can see what looks like a deep canyon. From Mars, the sun looks smaller and fainter than on Earth. As it sets, you can see two small moons in the sky above.

Mars

Mars, sometimes called the Red Planet, is relatively close to Earth. Mars is smaller than Earth but larger than Mercury. Its atmosphere is thin and contains no oxygen, and humans can't breathe it. It's likely that there was liquid water on Mars many years ago. This means that life could have developed there. Mars may, in fact, still be home to simple life forms. A person would weigh about the same on Mars as on Mercury, much less than on Earth.

The poles of Mars are covered with a thick layer of white frost — frozen carbon dioxide and a little water.

The temperatures on Mars are low. The daytime temperature on the Martian equator may be as high as a cold winter day on Earth, but for most of the planet it is much colder, averaging about 70 degrees below zero.

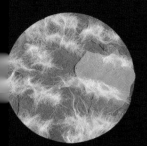

Earth

Mars

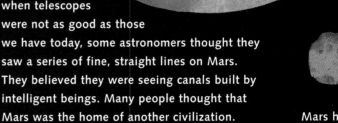

Day and night on Mars are almost the same length as on Earth. The Martian "day" is 37 minutes longer than an Earth day.

A car trip to Mars, at 60 miles per hour, would take 90 years.

Years ago, when telescopes were not as good as those we have today, some astronomers thought they saw a series of fine, straight lines on Mars. They believed they were seeing canals built by intelligent beings. Many people thought that Mars was the home of another civilization. Eventually, better telescopes showed that the lines — and canals — did not really exist.

Mars has two small moons, called Deimos and Phobos, each only a few miles across.

We have sent several probes to Mars. Some of them, like the Mars rover, have landed, explored the surface, and sent back pictures and information.

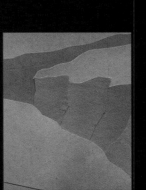

Valles Marineris is an enormous chasm, 2,500 miles long and up to 6 miles deep. It is one of the most prominent features on Mars.

The largest volcano on any planet, Maxwell Mons rises 15 miles above the plains of Mars. Mount Everest, the tallest mountain on Earth, is less than 6 miles high.

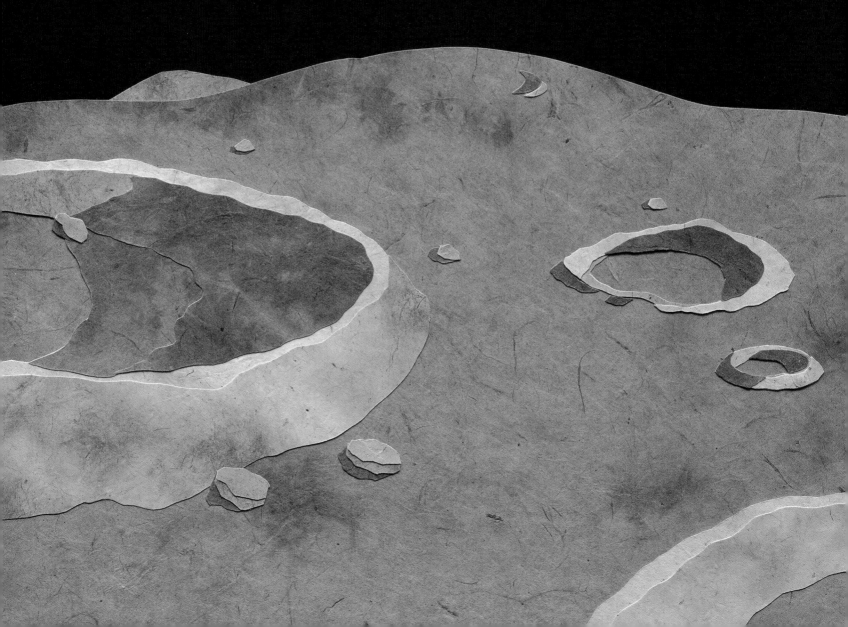

Walking across the barren surface of Ceres, the largest asteroid, you notice how little you weigh. A step sends you to a height of 75 feet, and you drift slowly back down. The landscape on Ceres reminds you of that on the moon: soft, dusty soil spread over a hilly land covered with craters. There is no air here, and it is very cold. When you visit Ida, a much smaller, potato-shaped asteroid, you find a surface like that of Ceres. Here you weigh only a few ounces. You must be careful as you walk, or you will launch yourself into space and never return.

Asteroids

There are hundreds of thousands of asteroids. All of them combined would make a body smaller than the moon.

Most asteroids revolve around the sun in paths that lie between the orbits of Mars and Jupiter. They are made of material left over from the formation of the planets. There have been collisions between asteroids, and many of the ones you now see are pieces of once-larger asteroids.

Asteroids are made of rock. No asteroid has an atmosphere.

This is Ceres, the largest asteroid, which is about 600 miles in diameter. The second largest is Pallas, about 360 miles in diameter. Third and fourth largest are Vesta and Hygiea. All the other asteroids are less than 210 miles across. Thousands of asteroids have been cataloged, and we can be sure that many more have not yet been detected.

Ida   Pallas   Ceres

Here Ida, Pallas, and Ceres are compared with Earth.

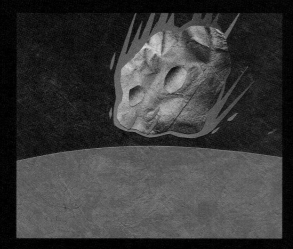

Some asteroids have orbits that bring them close to Earth. Every so often, an asteroid collides with our planet. These collisions can cause incredible damage, sometimes killing most of the living things on Earth. Fortunately, such big collisions are rare. They normally happen only once in tens of millions of years.

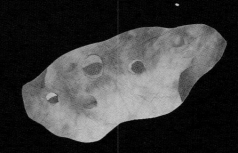

The asteroid Ida is not spherical. It is lumpy and irregularly shaped, like a potato. There is a tiny moon in Ida's sky. This moonlet, Dactyl, is only about one mile in diameter.

Earth

As you get close to this giant planet, you see that what at first looked like the surface is really the tops of thick clouds. You feel very heavy. In fact, you weigh two and a half times more here than on Earth. Fast-moving, colorful bands of clouds race past below you, encircling the entire planet. As you pass through the layers of clouds — a white layer, an orange layer, then a blue layer — the light fades and the temperature rises. Occasionally a flash of lightning illuminates the clouds. The atmosphere becomes thicker and thicker until, gradually, it has become a liquid. This is not water, but an ocean of liquid hydrogen. If you could keep going, you'd finally arrive at the rocky core of Jupiter, where the pressure is enormous and it is hotter than the surface of the sun.

Jupiter

Jupiter is big. It's so big that more than 1,300 Earths would fit inside it. In fact, the fifth planet contains more than two-thirds of all the matter in the solar system outside of the sun. Seen from Earth, this giant planet is usually the fourth brightest object in the sky, after the sun, the moon, and Venus (sometimes Mars is brighter than Jupiter).

Here are Earth, the moon, and Jupiter's moons Ganymede and Europa compared to the giant planet.

Earth   Moon   Ganymede   Europa

At its closest, Jupiter is almost 400 million miles from Earth. If we were able to drive there in a car at 60 miles per hour, we'd arrive in about 740 years.

Jupiter has a very short day, rotating once every ten hours. A year on Jupiter — the time it takes the planet to complete a trip around the sun — lasts almost twelve Earth years.

Winds of up to 400 miles per hour blow across Jupiter. These winds create the planet's distinctive bands of clouds. Among these bands is a huge red spot, nearly three times the size of Earth. The Great Red Spot is a fierce storm that has raged for more than 300 years.

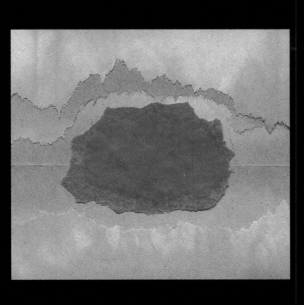

Jupiter has no solid surface, but if you could find a place to stand you'd discover that you are now much heavier. If you weigh 80 pounds on Earth, you'll weigh 188 pounds on Jupiter.

On Io, a large moon of Jupiter, you walk through a deep layer of ash that covers the surface. This fine ash varies in color from yellow to red to black. Here and there the ground is dusted with a layer of white frost — frozen sulfur dioxide. There are mountains all around, some of them volcanoes spewing lava. In the distance, a plume of yellow volcanic ash rises high above the surface. There may be as many as 300 volcanoes erupting at the same time on Io. Above, Jupiter shines brightly, filling a large part of the black sky. It is cold. There is no atmosphere, and no craters are visible — they have been buried beneath volcanic ash and lava.

The Moons of Jupiter

From a distance Europa appears to have veins over its surface, as if it were a living organism. A closer look shows that the surface is covered with ridges, valleys, complex patterns of lines and spots, and a few shallow craters. As on Io, there is no air here, and the temperature is very low. On the surface, a layer of fine soil covers a sheet of solid ice.

Io is the most volcanically active body in the solar system. One astronomer said the colorful splotches of volcanic ash make this moon look like a pizza.

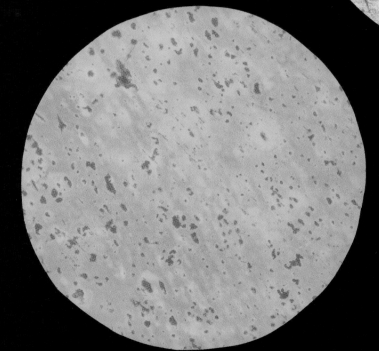

There is a chance that boring through Europa's thick crust of ice will reveal some form of life living in an ocean that could be many miles deep. This ocean is heated by tides created by Jupiter's enormous gravity. Liquid water and some form of energy, like this tidal heating, are essential to the development of life as we know it.

Jupiter has dozens of moons, and more are being discovered all the time. Most of these newly discovered moons are tiny, only a few miles in diameter.

The four largest and best known of Jupiter's moons are called the Galilean moons, discovered in the 1600s by the scientist Galileo. They are named Callisto, Ganymede, Europa, and Io. All are about the size of Earth's moon or slightly larger.

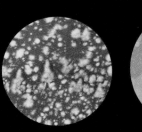

Callisto

Ganymede

Europa

Io

Earth's moon

From far away, Saturn's ring system is awesomely beautiful. As you get closer the view becomes even more splendid. Saturn shines as a bright yellowish ball, surrounded by colorful, flat rings that extend far from its surface. Passing through the rings, you can see that they are made of millions of small rocks and chunks of ice that range from the size of a pea to the size of a house. There are so many pieces so close together that from a distance they seem to form a solid sheet. Below the rings, near the top of the clouds that cover Saturn, you enter a thick layer of haze that dims your view of the cloud layers below. Behind you the sun shines weakly. Here you weigh about the same as on Earth, but the temperature is very low, colder than anywhere on our planet. As you descend, you pass through several layers of clouds, and the temperature and pressure gradually increase. If you were to keep going, you'd reach a rocky core deep within the planet. Here on Saturn the days pass more quickly than on Earth — a full day is only about ten hours long, about the same as on Jupiter.

Saturn

Saturn, the sixth planet, is twice as far away from the sun as Jupiter. It is the second largest planet, so large that almost 800 Earths would fit inside it. Saturn is a gas giant, and it is much less dense than Earth. In fact, Saturn would float on water.

Here are the Earth and Saturn's moon Titan shown at the same scale as Saturn.

There are more than 30 moons of Saturn. Many of these are quite small — just a few miles across.

Titan, the largest moon of Saturn, is about 3,000 miles in diameter. It's the biggest of all solar system moons except Jupiter's Ganymede. Titan is also the only moon in the solar system with an atmosphere. The temperature on Titan is very low, but there may be oceans of methane on the surface, which is always hidden by clouds. Scientists think that Titan is one of the places in the solar system that could possibly support life.

Though a day on Saturn is just ten hours long, a year here lasts 29 Earth years.

Traveling at 60 miles per hour, you would need 1,500 years to reach Saturn from Earth.

Saturn has three major rings and many smaller ones. Though the rings are many thousands of miles across, they are only a few hundred feet thick. This is very thin — the same proportion as a sheet of paper that is 100 yards across. The rings may be the remains of a shattered moon or other large object.

Uranus

From space, Uranus looks like a blue-green sphere, with a few dim points of light — its moons — and a faint set of rings closely encircling the planet. As you pass near the rings, you can see that they are made of chunks of rock and ice like the rings of Saturn. Like the other gas giants, Uranus is completely covered by clouds and has no visible solid surface. From here, the sun looks like a very bright star. As you plunge into the clouds, you pass through a blue-tinted layer of haze, then into clouds that are banded like those on Jupiter. As on the other gas giants, the temperature and pressure rise as you descend. If you could keep going you would eventually reach a small rocky core, as in Jupiter and Saturn.

Uranus

Earth   Titania

Uranus rotates once about every 16 hours. However, days, nights and seasons here are very strange. Depending on the season and where you are on the surface, daylight may last from 8 hours up to 42 Earth years. A year on Uranus is 84 Earth years long.

At the cloud tops the temperature is very low, about 330 degrees below zero. The sun provides less than 1 percent of the heat that it does at Earth's surface.

Uranus, the seventh planet, is four times as large as Earth, and almost twenty times as far from the sun. You weigh about the same here as you do on Earth.

A trip to Uranus at 60 miles per hour would take 3,200 years.

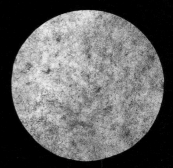

Uranus has more than 20 moons. Most of these are small, less than 100 miles across. The largest is Titania, about 1,000 miles in diameter, less than half the size of Earth's moon. It is made of ice and rock, and some astronomers have described it as a dirty ice ball.

Neptune

Neptune, the eighth planet, is almost a twin of Uranus. The clouds here look like those on Uranus, but have more of a bluish tint. Neptune is slightly smaller than Uranus, but it is denser. You weigh a little more here than on Earth. The sun looks like a bright star, and it provides little light or heat. At the cloud tops, the temperature is even colder than on Uranus. Neptune's moons look like faint points of light in the sky. Entering the atmosphere you are blown sideways by winds of up to 1,500 miles per hour, the fastest in the solar system. There is a deep layer of clouds on Neptune, and once again the temperature and pressure increase as you approach the planet's small, solid core.

At the cloud tops the temperature here is about 350 degrees below zero.

It would take 5,100 years to reach Neptune from Earth if you were traveling at 60 miles per hour.

A full cycle of day and night on Neptune lasts about 17 hours.

The plumes that are sometimes seen in the atmosphere of Neptune are probably clouds that form from rapidly rising gases, perhaps made of methane ice crystals. More common are white or pink clouds that form long streaks across the planet, looking like cirrus clouds on Earth.

There are faint rings around Neptune. Here and there the rings are brighter, where more material has accumulated.

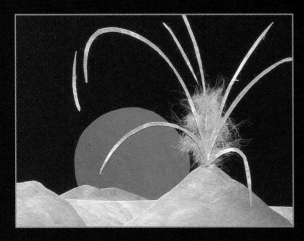

Neptune's largest moon, Triton, is smaller than Earth's. Triton's surface is very light in color, so it reflects most of the sunlight that hits it. This makes Triton the coldest place in the solar system, with an average temperature of almost 400 degrees below zero. There are ice volcanoes on Triton that erupt liquid gas instead of molten rock. It's so cold here that this liquid quickly freezes.

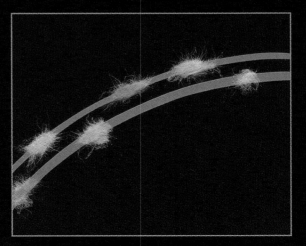

Neptune

Earth   Triton

From a distance, Pluto looks like a double planet. Its moon, Charon, is about half the size of the planet itself. The planet's surface shows broad light and dark areas. Pluto is the most distant of the planets, but it is solid, not made of gas like the other outer planets. Once on the surface, you find a cold, barren plain. Hills and a few craters are nearby. It is extremely cold here. You've arrived as Pluto's orbit is taking it further from the sun, and you can see Pluto's thin atmosphere freezing and falling to the ground like snow. From here the sun is simply another star, providing almost no light or heat. You have a clear view of Charon, which seems to hover overhead. It looks more than six times as large as the moon does from Earth.

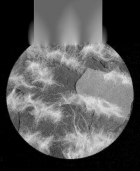

Earth

Pluto   Charon

When Pluto is farther from the sun, its surface is bright. As the planet moves closer to the sun, the light-colored frozen atmosphere covering its surface melts, and Pluto appears to get darker.

A day on Pluto is six and a half Earth days long, and a year here is 248 Earth years long.

The travel time to Pluto from Earth at 60 miles per hour is about 6,800 years.

When Pluto is nearest the sun, it is closer than Neptune. When it is most distant from the sun, it is about two billion miles beyond Neptune. The two planets cannot collide, however, because Pluto's orbit is tilted, causing it to pass above or below Neptune. Because of this unusual orbit and its small size, some astronomers believe that Pluto is not really a planet.

Charon revolves around Pluto in such a way that it always stays above the same spot on Pluto's surface. This means that on one side of Pluto Charon is always visible, while on the other side Charon is never seen.

Comets

You've decided to visit Halley's comet. It is the best known of the comets, because it can be seen clearly from Earth when its orbit brings it near the sun every 76 years. Halley's comet will come back next in about the year 2060. You arrive at the comet when it is most distant from the sun, beyond the orbit of Neptune. The comet's surface is black and rough, and it is very cold. Halley's is a typical comet, about ten miles long and five miles wide. Standing on the comet, you weigh about the same as a paper clip on Earth. You must move very carefully so you don't float away into space. The comet begins to warm up as it moves toward the sun. If you stay here long enough, about 35 years, you'll notice small jets of gas and dust beginning to erupt from the surface. The heat from the sun is starting to boil off some of the ice inside. As the comet gets closer to the sun, the material shooting from the surface forms a large cloud around the body of the comet and a long, pointed tail of dust and gas that points away from the sun. These clouds give comets their familiar appearance.

From just inside the orbit of Pluto to far beyond lie two regions of space called the Oort cloud and the Kuiper (pronounced "Kyper") cloud. The more distant region, the Oort cloud, is home to millions of comets. The orbit of Pluto is in the inner part of the Kuiper cloud. In this region are hundreds of asteroid-size objects. They are probably made of rock and ice, and some may be as large as Pluto.

Comets are made of dust and rock fragments held together by ice.

The solar system is enormous, with travel between planets requiring months or years, even at speeds of thousands of miles per hour. Once you leave the solar system behind and head out toward the stars, things get even more spread out.

Our sun is a star. There are billions of other stars, but they are very far away. The distances between the stars are so great that a different way of measuring distance — light-years — is used.

The fastest speed we know is that of light, which moves so quickly it can travel around the world seven times in one second. The distance light travels in one year, about six trillion miles, is called a light-year. Light takes only eight minutes to travel from the sun to Earth, and about five and a half hours to get from Pluto to Earth. The nearest star, Proxima Centauri, is so far away that its light takes four years to get to Earth. A spaceship traveling 40,000 miles per hour could reach Pluto in ten years, but it would take 68,000 years to get to Proxima Centauri. And this is the nearest star!

Beyond the Solar System

Stars aren't spread out evenly in space. Billions
of them group together in clusters called galaxies.
Our sun is in a galaxy called the Milky Way
because we see it as a faint, milky streak across
the sky. Without a telescope, we can see only a
few thousand stars from Earth, but the Milky Way
contains perhaps 100 billion stars.

The solar system is about here, out near one edge
of the Milky Way, far from the center. It takes
light 100,000 years to travel from one side of our
galaxy to the other.

There are thousands of millions of other galaxies
beyond our own, each with thousands of millions
of stars. The nearest major galaxy is so far away
that its light takes more than two million years to
reach us.

The simplest space travel is an orbit around Earth. This is what the astronauts in the space station are doing. If you join them you'll find yourself floating around inside the cabin — you'll be "weightless." Objects you hold and release, even a glass of water, will stay suspended in midair. Outside, there is no air, so you are relying on the space station to support your life. Far below you can see clouds, oceans, and continents. At night, you can see the lights of cities and highways. It takes just 90 minutes to circle Earth, which means you are moving 17,000 miles per hour. To move beyond Earth's orbit, you must travel even faster to escape Earth's gravity — about 25,000 miles per hour.

Space Travel

The nearest body in space is the moon, about 240,000 miles away. The moon is the only place outside Earth that has been visited by astronauts. Without wind or water to erode them, their footprints will remain on the dusty surface for thousands of years.

Humans face many dangers in space. Radiation from the sun isn't blocked by a magnetic field and atmosphere the way it is on Earth and can damage the body's cells and cause sickness or death. Meteors, even very tiny ones, are like bullets that can punch holes in a spacecraft. And spending a long time in zero gravity can cause a space traveler's muscles and organs to become very weak.

The next place humans are likely to visit is Mars. To get there you'll probably travel at around 30,000 miles per hour, which will get you there in about six months. That's a long time to stay inside a small cabin, living off the food, water, and air you are taking with you.

After landing on Mars, you are able to explore for about a year and a half. By that time, Mars and Earth will be positioned in their orbits so that a simple path back to Earth is possible. The entire trip takes about three years.

If you want to travel to more distant planets, much more time is needed. To visit Pluto and its moon, Charon, you'll be traveling ten to twenty years in each direction.

The stars are thousands of times as far away as Pluto, so you will not be traveling there unless a much faster means of travel is discovered. Travel across our galaxy or to other galaxies would require enormous lengths of time. At the speed of light, it would take 30,000 years to reach the center of our galaxy. Andromeda, the nearest major galaxy, would take more than two million years to reach. If you are traveling at 30,000 miles per hour, the speed of a planetary probe in the solar system, then the travel time to Andromeda is greater than the

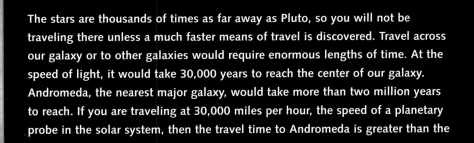

Earth is covered with life. From giant mammals to one-celled bacteria, from huge redwood trees to tiny plankton in the sea, life is everywhere. Bacteria, worms, and other forms of life have even been found near volcanic vents, called black smokers, deep in the Earth's oceans. There is almost no oxygen here and the water temperature can be hundreds of degrees. This could mean that life might exist in the extreme conditions found on some other planets and moons. The only other place people have visited is our moon, where there is no air, no water, and the temperature is either very hot or very cold. There is no sign of life there. The same conditions are found on Mercury, making it very unlikely that life can exist there either. Venus is extremely hot and has no water. Likewise, there is no liquid water or air on the asteroids, on the moons of Mars, or on those of Uranus, Neptune, or Pluto. Jupiter, Saturn, Uranus, and Neptune all have crushing atmospheres, little water vapor, and surfaces that are very hot and at tremendous pressures. Pluto is so cold that air itself can freeze. It seems that only on Mars, one or two of Jupiter's moons, and perhaps one moon of Saturn is there a possibility of finding life as we know it.

Tube worms living near volcanic vents on the Earth's seafloor. If life can survive here, perhaps it can be found elsewhere in the solar system.

Life in the Solar System

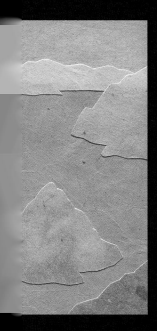

Mars has no liquid water now, but channels and other features show that water may have flowed on the surface in the past. Mars has a thin atmosphere and temperatures that are colder than those on Earth, but the planet may be warm enough to sustain life. If life does not exist now on Mars, it may have at one time.

In the past, science fiction stories were filled with strange creatures that inhabited the planets, especially Mars and Venus. One famous tale by H. G. Wells told of the invasion of Earth by Martians. We know now that creatures like us could not survive anywhere else in the solar system. It is possible, however, that simple forms of life, perhaps very different from any we know, will be found on one of the more sheltered solar system environments.

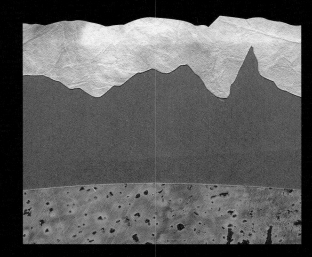

Europa and perhaps one or two other large moons of Jupiter have a surface of ice that may cover an ocean of water. Life of some sort may have evolved in these seas.

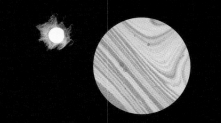

What about life beyond our solar system? We know that some other stars have planets. It may be that there are billions of other solar systems, many with planets somewhat like our own. Could there be life on one of these worlds? No one knows, and the great distances involved make it hard to find out. Even if we discovered a civilization somewhere else in our galaxy, it could take many thousands of years, each way, to send messages back and forth.

Over the past fifty years, many people have reported seeing flying saucers or aliens. Some have even claimed to have been kidnapped by creatures from space. So far, no scientific evidence exists to support any of these claims.

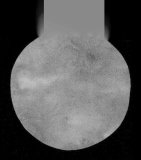

Titan, a satellite of Saturn, has an atmosphere. It is very cold on Titan, and the composition of the atmosphere is much different from that of Earth's, but there could be a form of life there unlike any we are familiar with.

Astronomers and other scientists are continuing to plan the exploration of the solar system. Some of these explorations will involve unmanned probes, but humans may also visit asteroids or travel to other moons and planets. They will be trying to understand how the solar system formed and what will happen to it in the future. They will also be looking for signs of life. The discovery of life beyond Earth would be perhaps the greatest achievement of science

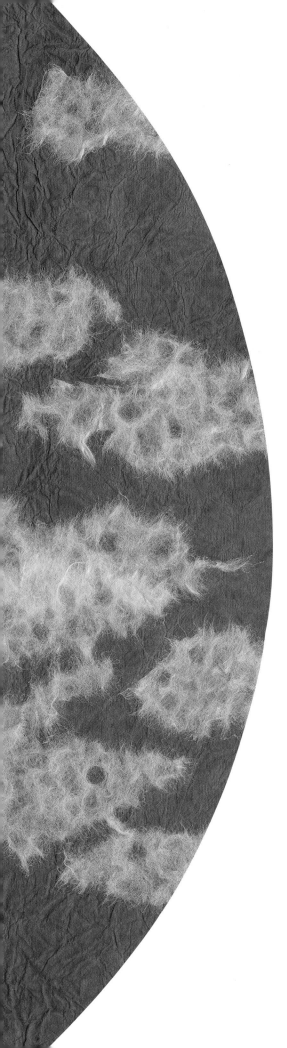

For Margaret

— AWJ

For Jamie

— SWJ

Bibliography and additional information:

Tim Furniss, *Atlas of Space Exploration*.
London, UK, Z-Publishing Ltd., 2001.

John Gribbin and Simon Goodwin, *Empire of the Sun*.
New York, New York University Press, 1998.

Carl Sagan, *Pale Blue Dot*.
New York, Ballantine, 1994.

Seymour Simon, *Destination Jupiter*.
New York, Morrow Junior Books, 1998.

F.W. Taylor, The Cambridge Photographic Guide to the Planets.
Cambridge, UK, Cambridge University Press, 2001.

There are many excellent Web sites with pictures and information about the solar system that are updated frequently. The NASA site, in particular, is very good:

http://www.jpl.nasa.gov/solar_system

Web site addresses often change. Find other sites by looking for "solar system facts" in Google or another search engine.

Text copyright © 2004 by Alvin Jenkins
Illustrations copyright © 2004 by Steve Jenkins

www.houghtonmifflinbooks.com

The text of this book is set in Palatino and Syntax Bold.
The illustrations are collages of cut and torn paper.

Library of Congress Cataloging-in-Publication Data
Jenkins, Steve, 1952–
Next stop, Neptune : experiencing the solar system / by Steve Jenkins.
p. cm.
ISBN 0-618-41603-X
1. Solar system—Juvenile literature. I. Title.
QB501.3.J46 2004   523.2—dc22   2004005233

Printed in Singapore
TWP 10 9 8 7 6 5 4 3 2 1